A PORTRAIT OF
LINCOLN

A PORTRAIT OF
LINCOLN

JANET and PETER ROWORTH

HALSGROVE

First published in Great Britain in 2005

Copyright words © Janet and Peter Roworth 2005
Photographs © Roworth Images 2005

Title page photograph: *The Lincoln Imp, the famous carving in the cathedral's Angel Choir.*

British Library Cataloguing-in-Publication Data
A CIP record for this title is available from the British Library

ISBN 1 84114 453 3

HALSGROVE
Halsgrove House
Lower Moor Way
Tiverton, Devon EX16 6SS
Tel: 01884 243242
Fax: 01884 243325
email: sales@halsgrove.com
website: www.halsgrove.com

Printed and bound by D'Auria Industrie Grafiche Spa, Italy

INTRODUCTION

We have been visiting Lincoln for over thirty years, and are always thrilled when we drive over Pelham Bridge and see the cathedral towering above us. There can surely be no other city in the country where the cathedral exerts such a powerful dominance.

Wherever you are, if you look up, the towers are visible on the skyline. We are continually amazed that our medieval ancestors, with the most basic of tools, could create something so magnificent. It is certainly the jewel in Lincoln's crown, but as this book will hopefully show, the city has much more to offer.

The strategic potential of the site was first recognised by the Romans who established a fortress on the hilltop. As their armies moved northwards, the civilian settlement expanded down the slope to the river, while a commercial suburb developed beyond.

Soon after William the Conqueror's invasion of 1066, the Normans built first a castle and then a cathedral as they exerted their authority over the local population. Building work on the cathedral continued for several centuries as the original structure was re-built and enlarged. In the medieval period Lincoln was one of the most important cities in the country, with much of its wealth generated by the wool and cloth trades.

Visitors to the historic 'upper town' can walk around the cathedral, along the walls and towers of the Norman castle with superb views over the city, and through the impressive ruins of the medieval Bishops' Palace. They can wander along Bailgate, around the Cathedral Close and descend Steep Hill, surrounded by beautiful old buildings, many of which now house craft and gift shops, galleries and restaurants.

The nineteenth century was the great era of railways and steam-power, when several foundries and engineering works were established in the city. Along with their commercial and retail developments, the Victorians provided housing for the growing population of workers, schools, an art gallery, a library, and a public park. Many of these buildings can still be found in the 'lower town'. Here the busy High Street has local markets alongside modern shopping developments with a range of major retailers. The vibrant Brayford Waterfront, once the site of wharves and warehouses, has been redeveloped with new university buildings and an array of leisure and entertainment facilities.

We have really enjoyed exploring Lincoln, capturing the best of the old and the new, the well known and the less familiar. We hope that our personal selection of photographs will remind you of happy times you have spent in this beautiful city. Alternatively they may inspire you to come and search for your own favourite views or buildings.

Janet and Peter Roworth

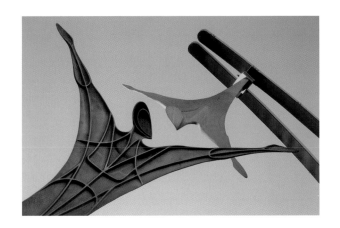

ACKNOWLEDGEMENTS

We wish to thank Roly Smith, editorial manager for Halsgrove, for his encouragement and guidance with this project.

Janet would like to thank the members of the Lincoln Local History Group for their interest, support and friendship over the past eight years.

The historical information within this book has been sourced from the second edition of *The Buildings of England: Lincolnshire* by Nicholas Pevsner and John Harris, revised in 1989 by Nicholas Antram, and from the details of Listed Buildings held as part of the Sites and Monuments Record by Lincolnshire County Council.

MAP OF LINCOLN

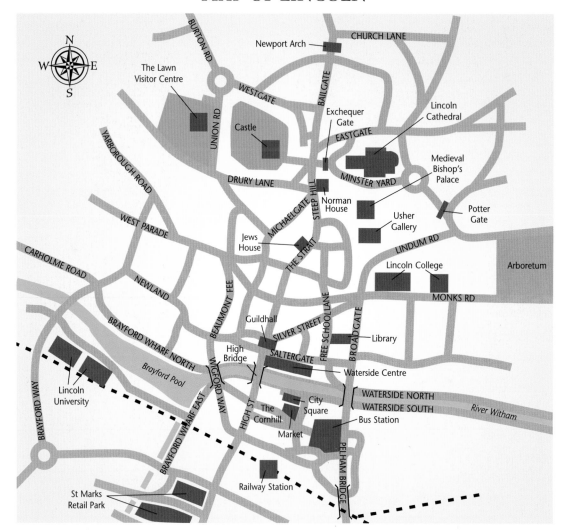

Opposite: **Lincoln Cathedral**
One of the finest medieval buildings in Europe, the spectacularly-situated cathedral towers over the city.

Romanesque frieze – cathedral

The twelfth-century frieze, currently undergoing restoration, is a kind of sculptural 'comic strip' running across the west front. It depicts scenes from the Bible, designed to instil fear and reverence.

Opposite: **West towers – cathedral**

The two west towers were heightened in the late fourteenth century. Originally they were topped with spires, but these were taken down in 1807 when they were found to be unsafe.

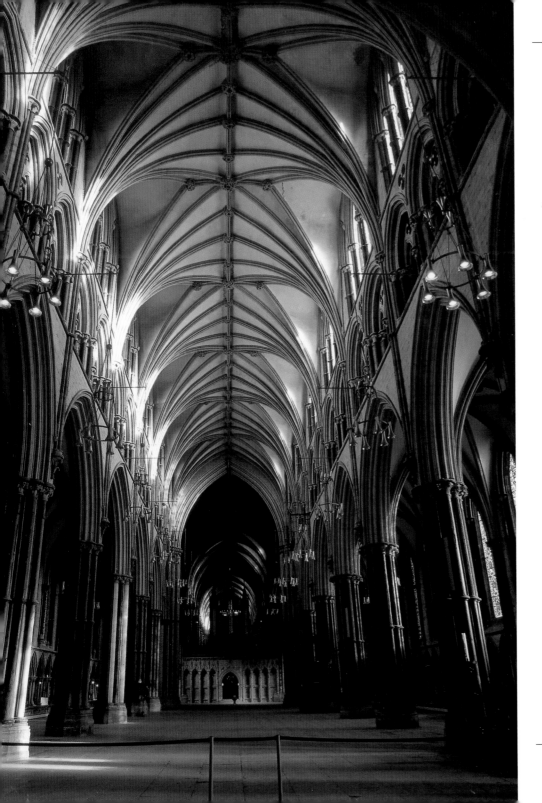

Nave – cathedral
The beautiful, light and spacious nave
is traditionally the public part of the
cathedral, now used for large services,
concerts and plays.

Bishop's Eye (exterior and interior) – cathedral
Dating from the fourteenth century, this
magnificent stained glass window in the south
transept takes its shape from two lime leaves,
and is a kaleidoscope of colour.

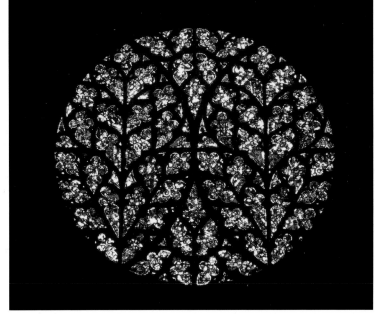

Cloister and library – cathedral

The cloister is a covered walkway around a central square garden. The Cathedral Library, designed by Sir Christopher Wren, was built over the north range of the cloister in the seventeenth century.

Cloister mural – cathedral
This large mural depicting the hillside location of the city of Lincoln was designed by
Carly Laking and executed by Art and Design students and tutors from the University of Lincoln.
It successfully screened the building work which was underway in the cloister.

Chapter House – cathedral (interior)
The slender central pier supports the vaulted
roof of the Chapter House, making it an attractive
venue for concerts and exhibitions.

Opposite: **Chapter House – cathedral (exterior)**
In this winter view, there is a dusting of snow on the
roof of the ten-sided meeting house, which played host to
the king and his parliament in the early fourteenth century.
It is still used for meetings of the General Chapter,
the governing body of the cathedral.

Exchequer Gate
This is the massive western gate of the Close, the enclosed area which once surrounded
the cathedral and now contains the houses and offices of its staff.

The 'Number Houses'
A picturesque group of Georgian houses within the Cathedral Close,
so called because they were the first in the city to be numbered.

Pottergate
As the lime trees on Minster Green shed their leaves they reveal these attractive buildings in the Cathedral Close.

The Chancery – Pottergate
This is the oldest brick building in the city, and was the home in the late fourteenth
century of Katherine Swynford, the mistress and later the wife of John of Gaunt.

Potter Gate
A restored fourteenth-century
gatehouse which once housed a
portcullis, Potter Gate is now closed
to the traffic which skirts around
its left side.

The Adam and Eve public house – Lindum Road
In Victorian times the landlord was forced to remove his new sign when
local officials took offence at the naked figures of Adam and Eve!

Tennyson statue – Minster Green
Created in 1905 by George Frederick
Watts, the Tennyson statue was placed
close to the north side of the cathedral.

Opposite:
Tennyson statue
Autumn leaves surround the statue
of Alfred Lord Tennyson, who is
shown with his wolfhound, Karenina.
Tennyson is holding a flower, and
the inscription on the statue reads:

Flower in the crannied wall,
I pluck you out of the crannies,
I hold you here, root and all, in my hand,
Little flower – but if I could understand
What you are, root and all, an all in all,
I should know what God and man is.

Lamp standard – Minster Green
One of the old gas lamp-posts cast at William Foster's Wellington Foundry in 1866. Fosters were important manufacturers of threshing machines and traction engines in the nineteenth and early-twentieth centuries.

Opposite:
Floral display – Exchequer Gate
Floral displays, sponsored by local companies, bring a splash of colour to the city during the summer months.

Bust of King George III – castle
Originally this bust was part of a full statue
of the king placed on top of Dunstan Pillar in 1810.
During the Second World War, the statue was removed
and the pillar re-sited and reduced in size by the R.A.F.

Opposite: **Gatehouse – castle**
This is the mighty eastern entrance to the castle,
built by William the Conqueror. The lawned grounds
are now used to host open-air entertainment events.

Old gaol – castle (front)
Dating from 1787, this building has been a debtors' prison and then the home of the prison governor.
Today it houses one of only four surviving copies of the Magna Carta, signed by King John in 1215.

Old gaol – castle (back)
The rear block of the prison was added in 1846 when prisoners were held in individual cells.
The exercise yard can be seen behind its high enclosing wall.

Crown Court – castle
A view from the Observatory Tower of the Crown Court building, Ellis's Windmill and the Vale of Trent beyond.

Cobb Hall – castle
In the first half of the nineteenth century, the county gallows were sited on the roof of this castle tower, in an era when public executions attracted large crowds of spectators.

Lucy Tower – castle
From 1824, the Lucy Tower became the burial place for prisoners who were executed or who died naturally while they were in prison. The simple gravestones are engraved with their initials.

**View over Castle Hill
to the cathedral**
The open space between the castle
and Exchequer Gate is not a hill, but
nevertheless it goes by the name Castle
Hill. A minibus waits to ferry less
able or energetic visitors between
the upper and lower parts of the city.

Leigh-Pemberton House – Castle Hill
The fine timber-framed building on the corner with Bailgate dates back to the sixteenth century.
It has been extensively restored and now serves as a Tourist Information Office.

The Magna Carta public house – Exchequer Gate
This public house is named after one of the most important documents in English history, the Magna Carta, a copy of which is on public view in the old gaol inside the castle. The post box dates from the reign of Queen Victoria.

City of Lincoln display board – Castle Hill
Visitors are guided around the city by these display panels, which also offer maps for sale.

Tourists in Bailgate
A group of tourists enjoy a guided walk around the cathedral quarter.

Roofs and chimneys – Bailgate
A view from the castle walls of the roofs and chimney pots in the Bailgate area of the city.

The White Hart Hotel – Bailgate
There has been a White Hart Inn in the city since the fifteenth century. Much of the present building dates from the eighteenth and nineteenth centuries, when it also had extensive stable yards to cater for travellers arriving by stagecoach.

Opposite: **Bailgate Kitchens – 4 Bailgate**
This picturesque shop front dates from the late eighteenth century.

BBC Radio Lincolnshire – Newport
Opened in 1939 as the Radion Cinema, this building is now home to BBC Radio Lincolnshire.

Newport
The tree-lined route heading north out of the city looks particularly attractive in autumn.

Newport Arch
Said to be the only Roman gateway in Britain still used by traffic, the archway is
astride Ermine Street and marked the northern edge of the Roman walled town.

Roman remains – City Hall
The remains of the Roman West
Gate in the lower city wall contrasts
with the concrete and glass of
the modern City Hall.

Bishops' Palace

The ruins of the once-impressive palace of the medieval
bishops of Lincoln are situated on the steep terraced
slopes below the cathedral. Bishop Alnwick added
the gatehouse tower in the fifteenth century.

Opposite: **Contemporary heritage garden – Bishops' Palace**
Opened in 2001, the design for this garden was inspired by
its historic setting at the Bishops' Palace. Nine hornbeam
trees are planted at the intersections of the lattice paths.

The Castle Hotel – Westgate
Originally the National School for the northern part of the city, this building has found a new use as an hotel.

Inscription on the Castle Hotel
The former National School was built in 1852.

Old sign for the city fire engine – Church Lane
The city's horse-drawn fire engine was formerly
located under this sign, while the police station
was in the adjacent part of the building, which
dates from 1880. The horse was reputedly
kept in the yard alongside.

The Lincoln Hotel – Eastgate
Designed in the 1960s, the hotel overlooks Minster Green.
The excavated remains of a Roman tower can be seen in front of the hotel.

Eastgate House – Eastgate
This attractive old brick property was re-fronted with Venetian windows
and an elegant portico in the eighteenth century.

Museum of Lincolnshire Life – Burton Road
Built in the nineteenth century as the barracks for the North Lincolnshire Militia,
this building is now a museum of social history and the Museum of the Royal Lincolnshire Regiment.

Ellis's Windmill – Mill Road

Once there were as many as nine windmills along The Cliff in Lincoln, all well-placed to catch the prevailing south-westerly winds. This is the only one to survive in full working order, the brick tower dating from 1798.

Water tower – Westgate
Thought by many to be the keep of
the castle, the water tower was cleverly
disguised behind its stone-faced walls.
It was built in 1911 as part of the
measures to improve the water supply
to the city, following a typhoid
epidemic in 1905.

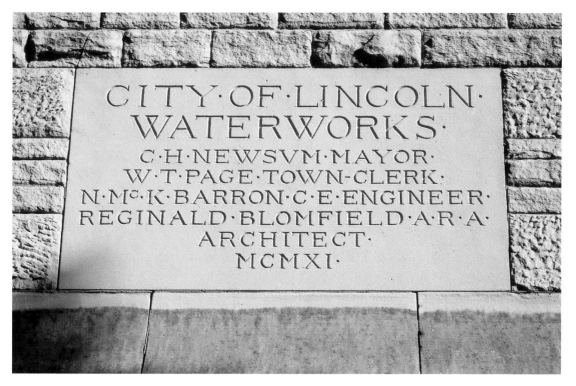

Inscription on the water tower
The officials responsible for building the water tower are
commemorated in this inscription, dated 1911.

THIS MONUMENT WAS ERECTED
TO COMMEMORATE THE
PIONEER WORK IN THE FIELD OF
MENTAL HEALTH OF
EDWARD PARKER
CHARLESWORTH M.D.
(DIED 21ST FEBRUARY 1853)
VICE PRESIDENT AND PHYSICIAN
THE LAWN HOSPITAL
FROM THE OPENING OF THE
HOSPITAL ON 9TH NOVEMBER 1819

The Lawn – Union Road

Opened in 1819 as the Lawn Hospital, a lunatic asylum catering for the mentally ill, the building is now a conference and banqueting centre. The Lincoln Archaeology Centre and Exhibition is also located within the complex.

Opposite: **Statue of Edward Parker Charlesworth M.D. – the Lawn**

The first physician at the Lawn Hospital, Dr Charlesworth practised an enlightened system of treatment, and this statue was erected to commemorate his pioneering work in the field of mental health.

**The Sir Joseph Banks
Conservatory – the Lawn**
The conservatory is dedicated to
the work of the Lincolnshire-born
plant hunter who accompanied
Captain James Cook on his voyage
of discovery to Australia in 1768.

De Wint House – Drury Lane and plaque
This was the Lincoln home of the artist
Peter de Wint and his brother-in-law
William Hilton. An important collection
of paintings by Peter de Wint is housed
in the Usher Gallery in the city.

PETER·DE·WINT
BORN·21·JANUARY·1784
DIED·30·JUNE·1849
MASTER·OF·THE·ART·OF
PAINTING·IN·WATER·COLOUR
IN·ASSOCIATION·WITH
HIS·BROTHER·IN·LAW
WILLIAM·HILTON·R·A·
BORN·IN·LINCOLN·3·JUNE·1786
DIED·30·DECEMBER·1839
KEEPER·OF·THE·ROYAL·ACADEMY
FROM·1827
PURCHASED·THE·SITE·IN·1814·AND
BUILT·THIS·HOUSE·WHEREIN·BOTH·LIVED
WHILE·RESIDENT·IN·LINCOLN

Steep Hill
Visitors to Steep Hill brave the cold wintry weather.

33 Steep Hill and plaque
Now Brown's Pie Shop, this
old property provided lodgings for
T.E. Lawrence (of Arabia) in 1923
when he was stationed at nearby
R.A.F. Cranwell.

Jelly and Chocolaterie – Steep Hill
A pair of gift shops on Steep Hill.

Norman House – Steep Hill
An important survival from the twelfth century, this stone building was once the home of a wealthy merchant.

Steep Hill
Visitors climb the narrow cobbled street of the aptly-named Steep Hill.

Opposite: **21-22 Steep Hill**
Once an inn by the name of the Harlequin, this is another timber-framed
building of the sixteenth century, standing on the corner of Michaelgate.

The Strait
Looking up the Strait on a damp autumn day with the central tower of the cathedral looming above.

Left and below: **Jew's House and Jews Court – the Strait**
The much-photographed Jew's House dates from the twelfth century and is a superb example of domestic architecture of the period. Jews Court on the right is the headquarters of the Society for Lincolnshire History and Archaeology.

Overleaf:
The Stonebow and Guildhall – High Street
There has been a gateway on this site since Roman times. The present building was completed in 1520, with the central arch intended for carriages and smaller pedestrian archways on each side. The upper floor houses the Guildhall, used by the City Council since the thirteenth century.

190-91 High Street
Designed by William Watkins in 1897, the entire façade of this High Street shop is faced in buff terracotta tiles, a material that had become very popular as it resisted the atmospheric pollution which was prevalent at the time.

2 Silver Street
The Curtis family has been
producing speciality foods, like
Lincolnshire Plumbread and
Lincoln Pork Pie, since 1828 for
their many customers in the
county and beyond.

Waterside Centre – Saltergate
Viewed across the churchyard garden of St Swithin, this modern shopping centre offers
visitors the chance to browse through a range of outlets in comfort, protected from the weather.

Waterside Centre – High Street
Escalators move shoppers effortlessly between
the two levels of the Waterside Centre.

High Bridge – High Street
One of the oldest bridges in
England which still supports
buildings, High Bridge spans the
River Witham. The stone arches
date from the Norman period while
the timbered buildings are
medieval in origin.

Tourist Information Office – Cornhill
This modern cast-iron shelter has been convincingly designed to appear Victorian.

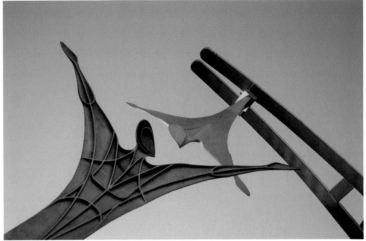

Empowerment sculpture
The powerful sculpture catches the
last rays of the evening sun.

Opposite: **Empowerment sculpture – City Square**
Turbine blades made in the city inspired this
Millennium sculpture by Stephen Broadbent.
It spans the River Witham in front of the
Waterside Centre, and stands 17 metres
(55 feet) high.

Corn Exchange

Once the upper floor was a bartering area for farmers and corn merchants, the Corn Exchange has now been turned into an attractive under-cover shopping centre. Market stalls are arranged under the glazed roof which extends around the building.

Corn Exchange
The pyramidal roof, topped by a wrought iron crest, was the main decorative feature of the 'new' Corn Exchange, built in 1879 to replace the smaller adjacent Old Corn Exchange.

City Square
Pigeons gather in City Square, one of the venues for outdoor markets.

Farmers' market – City Square
Farmers' markets have become a regular weekly event in the city, enabling shoppers
to purchase locally-produced fruit, vegetables, meat and dairy products.

Railway crossing – High Street
Lincoln is notable as the largest English city to still have traffic
on its main street interrupted by the regular passage of trains.

Central Station
This station was opened in 1848 serving the Great Northern Railway, but two years earlier St Mark's Station had opened for the rival Midland Railway. Central Station is the only one remaining operational today.

Former St Mark's Station
Closed in 1985, the old station building has been transformed into a spacious shop.
Inside an area has been set aside to explain its past.

St Mark's Retail Park
The old station yard has disappeared
to be replaced by modern retail units,
but the railway theme survives.

Debenhams – St Mark's Retail Park
An impressive modern design for this large departmental store.

Opposite: **Obelisk – St Mark's Retail Park**
This obelisk was originally sited on High Bridge but it was removed in 1939.
It reappeared in the 1980s as a centrepiece in the new St Mark's development.

Round House – High Street and plaque
This little building once accommodated
the level-crossing keeper for the railway
line heading into St Mark's Station.
Now it serves welcome refreshment
to visitors on foot.

The Ritz – High Street
The lighting and decoration of the bars and restaurant at the Ritz remind
visitors of the glamorous Art Deco style of the 1930s.

St Swithin's church –
Free School Lane
The tall spire of St Swithin's is a
prominent landmark in the lower
city. The church is the work of
James Fowler and it was largely
funded by the Shuttleworth family.

Central Methodist church – High Street

The bell tower, topped with an octagonal turret and spherical dome, is a decorative feature of this large Methodist chapel, built in 1905.

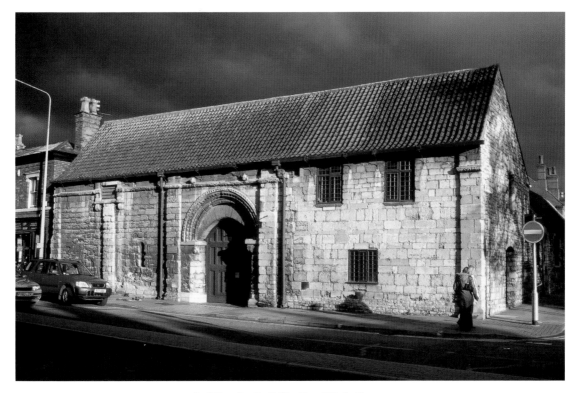

St Mary's Guildhall – High Street
Bathed in warm winter sunshine, this important Norman building
was used in the medieval period as the religious and social meeting place of
the wealthy cloth merchants of the Guild of St Mary.

Opposite: **St Peter at Gowts church – High Street**
This church and St Mary-le-Wigford further up the High Street are the two remaining
medieval parish churches in the city. Both have square Norman towers.

Brayford Pool
Once flanked by warehouses and busy wharves,
Brayford Pool is now home to pleasure boats and
canal barges. It is a natural basin at the junction
of the Rivers Witham and Till, and is linked to
the River Trent by the Fossdyke Canal.

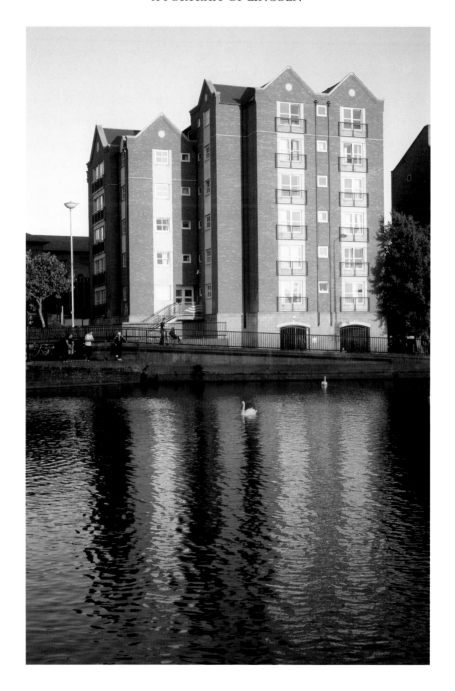

Odeon cinema – Brayford Wharf North
At night the Brayford waterfront comes alive with a range of bars, restaurants
and entertainment venues. The water reflects the brightly-lit Odeon cinema.

Opposite: **Grantavon House – Brayford Wharf East**
This modern apartment block is reflected in the waters of Brayford Pool.

Main building – University of Lincoln
The latest purpose-built university campus in the country was established on the southern edge of Brayford Pool.

Library – University of Lincoln
Opened in 2004, the university library is housed in a former sack
warehouse belonging to the Great Central Railway.

The Royal William IV public house – Brayford Wharf North
This public house is reputedly one of the oldest in the city, and must once have
provided refreshment to the dockworkers and boatmen on Brayford waterfront.

Wigford Way flyover
Signs on this bridge over the River Witham ask travellers 'Where are you going?' and 'Where have you been?'.

Usher Gallery – Lindum Road
Established in the 1920s to house the collection left to Lincoln Corporation by James Ward Usher, the gallery
also has paintings and drawings by Peter de Wint and a collection of memorabilia relating to Alfred Lord Tennyson.

'A Mighty Blow for Freedom' – Usher Gallery
Set in the Temple Gardens which surround the Usher Gallery, this modern sculpture
by Michael Sandle shows a large bronze figure smashing a television set.

Old gaol and Sessions House – Lindum Road
Opposite the gates of the Usher Gallery is the former prison and courthouse for the Quarter Session
courts, now converted into a restaurant run by the catering department of Lincoln College.

Lincoln Imp – Usher Gallery
This imp was found sitting on the gates of the Usher Gallery.
It became a popular symbol of Lincoln in the Victorian period when
James Usher, a local jeweller, was said to have made much
of his wealth by selling souvenir imps.

Lincoln Minster School – Lindum Road
These new school buildings at the top of Lindum Road have stunning views over the city.

1-2 Lindum Road
Pretty iron balconies decorate this house at the bottom of Lindum Road,
which was built in 1768 as the first Lincoln by-pass. It provided an alternative
route for carriages, avoiding the steep and narrow streets of the city centre.

Lincoln College – Monks Road
These new buildings for Lincoln College were
constructed on the site of the former cattle market.
The college is the largest educational institution
in the county, offering a wide range of vocational
and academic courses.

Gibney Building – Monks Road
Built as the Lincoln Science Day School, the fine façade is all that remains.
This is another building now occupied by students from Lincoln College.

Greestone Building – Lindum Road
Elaborate terracotta decoration on the face of this Victorian building, once the
Girls' High School but now part of the Cathedral Campus of the University of Lincoln.

**Former Wesleyan Day School –
Rosemary Lane**
Recently renovated, this former school
was established by the Wesleyan
Methodists in the nineteenth century.

Boys' entrance and girls' entrance
As seen here, boys and girls had separate
entrances into the school.

The Terrace – Arboretum – Monks Road
Opened in 1872, the Arboretum
was the first public park in the city.
The Terrace with its avenue of lime
trees was the most striking feature,
originally with a central conservatory.

Bandstand – Arboretum
Newly-restored in its original colours, this cast-iron bandstand
would have been the centrepiece for Sunday afternoon concerts.

PRESENTED BY F.J.CLARKE LINCOLN 1972

Lion statue – Arboretum
The mayor of the city, Mr F.C. Clarke, presented this magnificent statue to the park at its opening.

Lamp standard – Arboretum
Modern lamp standards, found throughout the city centre, have been cleverly modelled on the old gas lamps.

The Green Dragon public house – Broadgate
Attractive timber-framing decorates this ancient public house.

Opposite: **Drill Hall – Broadgate**
Provided by the industrialist Joseph Ruston for the City Volunteers, this recently
restored former military hall now hosts an exciting events programme.

The Co-operative Society building – Free School Lane
Dating from 1888, this was part of an extensive range of buildings which ran onto Silver Street, all belonging to the Lincoln Equitable Co-operative Industrial Society. The society was formed in 1861 and its branches soon spread across the city.

Opposite: **Central Library – Free School Lane**
Winter sunshine highlights the domed entrance to Lincoln's main library, designed by
Sir Reginald Blomfield. Recently extended, it also houses the Tennyson Research Centre.

Footbridge – Broadgate
This footbridge crosses the busy dual carriageway on Broadgate.

View from the footbridge
The effort of walking to the top of
the footbridge is rewarded by this
fine view of the cathedral.

Cheviot Street, looking north

Opposite: **Cheviot Street, looking south**
One of the terraces of Victorian housing built off Monks Road
for the workers from the factories and foundries along the river.

Clayton and Shuttleworth – Waterside South
When Nathaniel Clayton and Joseph Shuttleworth went into partnership in 1842, one of the great Lincoln manufacturing firms was born, producing steam engines and threshing machines at its Stamp End Works.

Robey & Co. Ltd (inscription) – Canwick Road
Robey & Co., another great manufacturing concern in the city,
produced steam engines, winding gear and boilers at its Globe Works.

This page and opposite: **Doughty's Mill – Waterside South**
Dating from 1863, machinery in this mill was once used to crush linseed and extract the oil.
The six-storey grain store has now been converted into residential units.

Globe Works – Canwick Road
Once occupied by Robey's workforce, the Globe Works are now used by builders' merchants.

View over the city from the castle
This view, looking south-east, shows that manufacturing activity at Stamp End
continues today, with Siemens producing gas turbines for the world market.

5-15 Beaumont Fee
This terrace of houses with attractively-shaped gables proudly displays the name of its builder.

Opposite: **Inscription**
Charles Knowles Tomlinson built these houses in 1885.

Lincoln City Football Club – Sincil Bank
The Stacey West Stand opened in 1990 commemorates the names of two Lincoln City fans
who died in the terrible grandstand fire at Valley Parade, Bradford, in 1985.

**Lincolnshire Echo Stand –
Lincoln City Football Club**
The Lincoln City football team plays
under the nickname of 'The Imps'.

Opposite: **The sign of the Lincoln Imp
public house – Blankney Crescent**
This imp watches over the traffic entering
the city along Riseholme Road.

Tritton Road
Many large retailing outlets can be found along this modern road which was named
after William Tritton, the managing director of William Foster Ltd., who was
closely involved in the design of the first armoured tanks used in the First World War.

Pelham Bridge
Opened in 1958 by the Queen, the bridge spans the railway lines leading from Central Station.
Drivers entering the city from the south and travelling over the bridge have a stunning view of the cathedral.

Christmas shop window display

High Street
As daylight fades, the busy High Street is lit by the shop window displays and the overhead Christmas decorations.

Christmas Market – Castle Hill

Christmas Market – Castle Hill
The hugely-popular Christmas Market is set against the stunning backdrop of the
cathedral and castle. It was started to mirror the market taking place in Lincoln's twin
town of Neustadt in Germany, and is now one of the biggest tourist events in Europe.

Stallholder – Christmas Market
A stallholder sells Santa hats to the young-at-heart. Many of the
vendors dress in costume to add to the festive atmosphere.

Funfair – Christmas Market
Visitors to the Christmas Market also enjoy the attractions of the funfair.

View of the floodlit cathedral
A night-time view of the floodlit cathedral seen from the footbridge over Broadgate, while traffic streams underneath.